unleashed

25 AFFIRMATIONS TO REACH YOUR FULL POTENTIAL

DALE A. O'SHIELDS

Elizabeth,
May God bless you!
-Dale O.
Jer 29:11

Published in Gaithersburg, Maryland, by COR Publishing. ISBN 978-0-9984731-1-6

Learn more about the author at www.daleoshields.com.

Printed in the United States of America

Unleashed:
"let loose, released, set free, unloosed, untied, unchained"

INTRODUCTION

Positive changes happen in us when we know, believe, confess and obey God's Word. When we agree with what God says about us, our minds are renewed, and our choices and habits improve.

One of the best ways to understand God's perspective about you is through the daily confession of His Word. Speaking His Word, and the truths it contains, over your life daily dismantles wrong thinking and develops right thinking. Speaking God's Word tears down destructive spiritual and mental strongholds and builds holiness, wholeness and wholesomeness in you. Right thinking is the key to right living.

This is the principle of biblical meditation. Its power and practice are emphasized throughout Scripture:

> Keep this Book of the Law always on your lips; meditate on it day and night, so that you may be careful to do everything written in it. Then you will be prosperous and successful. Joshua 1:8 NIV

> I meditate on your precepts and consider your ways. Psalms 119:15 NIV

> And now, dear brothers and sisters, one final thing. Fix your thoughts on what is true, and honorable, and right, and pure, and lovely, and admirable. Think about things that are excellent and worthy of praise. Philippians 4:8 NLT

In this book are 25 powerful affirmations based on biblical principles. These represent the way we are to think about God, ourselves, others, and the world.

Start confessing these over your life consistently. Declare these statements in faith, knowing that they represent who God has made and called you to be. Speak them confidently and out loud to yourself each day. While it may seem awkward and possibly even superficial initially, over time God's Word will get into your heart in a new way. It will change the way you think and live. The promise of Romans 12:2 will become real in your life.

> Don't copy the behavior and customs of this world, but let God transform you into a new person by changing the way you think. Then you will learn to know God's will for you, which is good and pleasing and perfect. Romans 12:2 NLT

Get ready, your life is about to change for the better!

1

In faith and with a heart to obey,
I confidently declare:

**I am a new creation in Jesus Christ.
Old things have passed away
and all things are new in my life.**

This means that anyone who belongs to Christ has become a new person. The old life is gone; a new life has begun!
2 Corinthians 5:17 NLT

Since you have heard about Jesus and have learned the truth that comes from him, throw off your old sinful nature and your former way of life, which is corrupted by lust and deception. Instead, let the Spirit renew your thoughts and attitudes. Put on your new nature, created to be like God—truly righteous and holy. Ephesians 4:21-24 NLT

It is essential that we know and accept the reality of salvation. When you receive Jesus Christ as your Savior, you are "born again." You are not the same person anymore. Something has radically changed within you. Knowing that you are a new creation helps you to live as a new creation.

What God is speaking to me:

2

In faith and with a heart to obey, I confidently declare:

**I am dead to sin,
and I am alive to God and to
His righteousness.**

In the same way, you also should consider yourselves dead to sin but alive for God in Christ Jesus. Now that you have been set free from sin, you have become slaves of righteousness. Romans 6:11, 18 CEB

God made him who had no sin to be sin for us, so that in him we might become the righteousness of God.
2 Corinthians 5:21 NIV

My old self has been crucified with Christ. It is no longer I who live, but Christ lives in me. So I live in this earthly body by trusting in the Son of God, who loved me and gave himself for me. Galatians 2:20 NLT

So I say, let the Holy Spirit guide your lives. Then you won't be doing what your sinful nature craves. Galatians 5:16 NLT

> While it is true that believers in Jesus still battle with sin and the sinful nature, we now have power over it. Sin no longer is the boss of us! We are free to do what is right rather than wrong.

What God is speaking to me:

3

In faith and with a heart to obey, I confidently declare:

**I am loved—personally loved—
by God. My sins are forgiven.
My guilt and shame are removed.
My past is covered. I am accepted.
I am not condemned.**

What happiness for those whose guilt has been forgiven! What joys when sins are covered over! What relief for those who have confessed their sins and God has cleared their record. Psalm 32:1-2 TLB

So now there is no condemnation for those who belong to Christ Jesus. Romans 8:1 NLT

Because of his love he had already decided to adopt us through Jesus Christ. He freely chose to do this so that the kindness he had given us in his dear Son would be praised and given glory. Through the blood of his Son, we are set free from our sins. God forgives our failures because of his overflowing kindness. Ephesians 1:5-7 GW

No, dear brothers and sisters, I have not achieved it, but I focus on this one thing: Forgetting the past and looking forward to what lies ahead, I press on to reach the end of the race and receive the heavenly prize for which God, through Christ Jesus, is calling us. Philippians 3:13-14 NLT

But if we confess our sins to him, he is faithful and just to forgive us our sins and to cleanse us from all wickedness. 1 John 1:9 NLT

> Nothing destroys present confidence more than guilt and shame from the past. Declaring and believing the truth of God's Word about His forgiveness frees us to live joyously in the present and to enthusiastically pursue the future.

What God is speaking to me:

4

In faith and with a heart to obey, I confidently declare:

The Lord is my Shepherd. I lack nothing. He causes me to lie down and feed in green pastures. He leads me to and allows me to drink from still, refreshing waters. He makes me whole. He guides me in paths of righteousness for His name's sake. I fear no evil. God is with me. He comforts me. He prepares a table for me in the presence of my enemies. He anoints my head with oil. My cup overflows. Goodness and mercy follow me all the days of my life. I dwell in God's house forever.

The Lord is my shepherd, I lack nothing. He makes me lie down in green pastures, he leads me beside quiet waters, he refreshes my soul. He guides me along the right paths for his name's sake. Even though I walk through the darkest valley, I will fear no evil, for you are with me; your rod and your staff, they comfort me. You prepare a table before me in the presence of my enemies. You anoint my head with oil; my cup overflows. Surely your goodness and love will follow me all the days of my life, and I will dwell in the house of the Lord forever. Psalm 23:1-6 NIV

The assurance of God's providential presence and care is important to our spiritual and emotional health. As a part of God's family, we are part of His sheepfold. As the Good Shepherd, He faithfully watches over us.

What God is speaking to me:

5

In faith and with a heart to obey, I confidently declare:

I ask God to fill me with His Holy Spirit, and He fills me. He promised that He would give the Holy Spirit to any and all who ask. I ask and He fills. I am powered by the Holy Spirit.

If you then, though you are evil, know how to give good gifts to your children, how much more will your Father in heaven give the Holy Spirit to those who ask him! Luke 11:13 NIV

Don't be drunk with wine, because that will ruin your life. Instead, be filled with the Holy Spirit. Ephesians 5:18 NLT

But you will receive power when the Holy Spirit comes upon you. And you will be my witnesses, telling people about me everywhere—in Jerusalem, throughout Judea, in Samaria, and to the ends of the earth. Acts 1:8 NLT

Too often we battle feelings of powerlessness. A sense of powerlessness breeds another dreadful feeling—hopelessness. God wants you to know His power is available and promised to all who ask Him for it. This gives us great hope.

What God is speaking to me:

6

In faith and with a heart to obey, I confidently declare:

God hears and answers my prayers according to His perfect will and timing. I only want what God wants for my life, because what God wants for me is always superior and unimaginably better than anything I could dream of or desire.

Keep on asking, and you will receive what you ask for. Keep on seeking, and you will find. Keep on knocking, and the door will be opened to you. For everyone who asks, receives. Everyone who seeks, finds. And to everyone who knocks, the door will be opened. Matthew 7:7-8 NLT

"Have faith in God," Jesus answered. "Truly I tell you, if anyone says to this mountain, 'Go, throw yourself into the sea,' and does not doubt in their heart but believes that what they say will happen, it will be done for them. Therefore I tell you, whatever you ask for in prayer, believe that you have received it, and it will be yours. And when you stand praying, if you hold anything against anyone, forgive them, so that your Father in heaven may forgive you your sins."
Mark 11:22-25 NIV

Now glory be to God, who by his mighty power at work within us is able to do far more than we would ever dare to ask or even dream of—infinitely beyond our highest prayers, desires, thoughts, or hopes. Ephesians 3:20 TLB

This is the confidence we have in approaching God: that if we ask anything according to his will, he hears us. And if we know that he hears us—whatever we ask—we know that we have what we asked of him.
1 John 5:14-15 NIV

Prayer is a vital part of spiritual health and growth. God invites us to come to Him for fellowship, and to ask Him for help, answers, and breakthroughs. We can't pray well if we doubt the power of prayer. God wants to change your thinking about prayer so that you approach Him confidently and boldly, knowing that He answers.

What God is speaking to me:

7

In faith and with a heart to obey, I confidently declare:

Divine opportunities open for me. God desires to use me, and He divinely opens doors and gives opportunities to me that are uniquely designed for me so that I am used to help, bless, and add value to others in the advance of His Kingdom.

Surely, Lord, you bless the righteous; you surround them with your favor as with a shield. Psalms 5:12 NIV

For the Lord God is a sun and shield; the Lord bestows favor and honor; no good thing does he withhold from those whose walk is blameless. Psalms 84:11 NIV

But the good man walks along in the ever-brightening light of God's favor. Proverbs 4:18a TLB

See, I have placed before you an open door that no one can shut. Revelation 3:8b NIV

The Lord bless you and keep you; the Lord make his face shine on you and be gracious to you; the Lord turn his face toward you and give you peace. Numbers 6:24-26 NIV

You are not an accident. God designed you on purpose for a purpose. You can trust Him to open the right doors for you. And when He does, don't despise them. Be faithful and fruitful where He plants you.

What God is speaking to me:

8

In faith and with a heart to obey,
I confidently declare:

I walk in love. I give no place to resentment, grudges, bitterness, or offenses in my heart. I refuse to give the devil a foothold in my life through sinful anger.

And "don't sin by letting anger control you." Don't let the sun go down while you are still angry, for anger gives a foothold to the devil. Get rid of all bitterness, rage, anger, harsh words, and slander, as well as all types of evil behavior. Instead, be kind to each other, tenderhearted, forgiving one another, just as God through Christ has forgiven you. Ephesians 4:26-27, 31-32 NLT

Live a life filled with love, following the example of Christ. He loved us and offered himself as a sacrifice for us, a pleasing aroma to God. Ephesians 5:2 NLT

> There is no faster way to short-circuit and drain your spiritual power than through resentment, bitterness, and offenses of the heart. Shield yourself from these by choosing to forgive others quickly and fully.

What God is speaking to me:

9

In faith and with a heart to obey,
I confidently declare:

I am godly, righteous, holy, sanctified, and pure by faith because of what Jesus did for me. I choose to please God because I love God. The power of the Holy Spirit enables me to live honorably and obediently before God. I want nothing to do with evil or darkness; spirit, soul, mind, or body.

In the past, some of you were like that, but you were washed clean. You were made holy, and you were made right with God in the name of the Lord Jesus Christ and in the Spirit of our God. 1 Corinthians 6:11 NCV

This is the message God has given us to pass on to you: that God is Light and in him is no darkness at all. So if we say we are his friends but go on living in spiritual darkness and sin, we are lying. But if we are living in the light of God's presence, just as Christ does, then we have wonderful fellowship and joy with each other, and the blood of Jesus his Son cleanses us from every sin. If we say that we have no sin, we are only fooling ourselves and refusing to accept the truth. 1 John 1:5-8 TLB

Now may the God of peace make you holy in every way, and may your whole spirit and soul and body be kept blameless until our Lord Jesus Christ comes again. 1 Thessalonians 5:23 NLT

> Spiritual growth is a process of moving from darkness to light, deception to truth, and unrighteousness to righteousness. The more you identify with light, truth, and righteousness, the less of the opposites you will have in your life.

What God is speaking to me:

In faith and with a heart to obey,
I confidently declare:

I am gifted and anointed by God to fulfill the tasks and assignments I have been called by God to do. I am teachable, growing, open to learning and developing, hungry to gain knowledge, wisdom, and new skills that better equip me to do what God has assigned me to do.

There are different kinds of spiritual gifts, but the same Spirit is the source of them all. There are different kinds of service, but we serve the same Lord. God works in different ways, but it is the same God who does the work in all of us. A spiritual gift is given to each of us so we can help each other. 1 Corinthians 12:4-7 NLT

Now, it is God himself who has anointed us. And he is constantly strengthening both you and us in union with Christ. 2 Corinthians 1:21 TPT

For we are God's masterpiece. He has created us anew in Christ Jesus, so we can do the good things he planned for us long ago. Ephesians 2:10 NLT

Each of you has received a gift to use to serve others. Be good servants of God's various gifts of grace. 1 Peter 4:10 NCV

But grow in the grace and knowledge of our Lord and Savior Jesus Christ. To him be glory both now and forever! Amen. 2 Peter 3:18 NIV

God has a purpose and plan for your life. He has equipped you with gifts to fulfill His purpose and plan. You are gifted. Your gifts need to be grown, polished and developed. A teachable attitude allows your basic gifts to become usable gifts that bless others.

What God is speaking to me:

11

In faith and with a heart to obey, I confidently declare:

I am quick to repent when convicted of sin, error, poor judgment or failures. I willingly choose attitudes of humility and meekness and reject attitudes of pride and presumption.

Godly sorrow brings repentance that leads to salvation and leaves no regret, but worldly sorrow brings death.
2 Corinthians 7:10 NIV

But he gives us more grace. That is why Scripture says: "God opposes the proud but shows favor to the humble." Submit yourselves, then, to God. Resist the devil, and he will flee from you. Come near to God and he will come near to you. Wash your hands, you sinners, and purify your hearts, you double-minded. James 4:6-8 NIV

All of you, clothe yourselves with humility toward one another, because, "God opposes the proud but shows favor to the humble." Humble yourselves, therefore, under God's mighty hand, that he may lift you up in due time.
1 Peter 5:5b-6 NIV

While God loves us as we are, He's not content to leave us as we are. He is committed to helping us lay aside everything that hurts or hinders our lives. When God reveals our sins to us, it's never to condemn us but to correct us. Our quickness to repent moves us forward and keeps us from unnecessary pain.

What God is speaking to me:

12

In faith and with a heart to obey, I confidently declare:

I am a faithful servant and steward. My highest aim is to serve God and others humbly, lovingly, quietly, faithfully, blamelessly, and honorably without concern for recognition or rewards. I trust God for promotion. I trust God for fruitfulness and ministry results.

You will lead by a completely different model. The greatest one among you will live as the one who is called to serve others, because the greatest honor and authority is reserved for the one with the heart of a servant. For even the Son of Man did not come expecting to be served by everyone, but to serve everyone, and to give his life in exchange for the salvation of many. Matthew 20:26b-28 TPT

Be devoted to one another in love. Honor one another above yourselves. Never be lacking in zeal, but keep your spiritual fervor, serving the Lord. Romans 12:10-11 NIV

This I know: the favor that brings promotion and power doesn't come from anywhere on earth, for no one exalts a person but God, the true judge of all. He alone determines where favor rests. He anoints one for greatness and brings another down to his knees. Psalms 75:6-7 TPT

> There is no greater calling in God's Kingdom than being a servant. When we live with the perspective of a servant we're guarded from attitudes of pride and entitlement. We're also prepared for any assignment God has for us—great or small.

What God is speaking to me:

13

**In faith and with a heart to obey,
I confidently declare:**

____

I am a loving (identify your roles and responsibilities such as husband/wife, father/mother, son/daughter, employee, etc.).

____

____

____

____

Love is patient, love is kind. It does not envy, it does not boast, it is not proud. It does not dishonor others, it is not self-seeking, it is not easily angered, it keeps no record of wrongs. Love does not delight in evil but rejoices with the truth. It always protects, always trusts, always hopes, always perseveres. 1 Corinthians 13:4-7 NIV

Don't do anything for selfish purposes, but with humility think of others as better than yourselves. Instead of each person watching out for their own good, watch out for what is better for others. Philippians 2:3-4 CEB

Dear children, let's not merely say that we love each other; let us show the truth by our actions. 1 John 3:18 NLT

We all have roles and responsibilities in life. To do them well we must start and end with love. Love must be the motivation for all we do. Love isn't a feeling, it's a commitment always to seek the best for others. God is love and grants us the ability to love.

What God is speaking to me:

14

In faith and with a heart to obey, I confidently declare:

I am disciplined in body, soul, mind, and spirit. I say "yes" to things that are good, right, honorable, healthy, wholesome, and helpful and "no" to the things that are not.

You've all been to the stadium and seen the athletes race. Everyone runs; one wins. Run to win. All good athletes train hard. They do it for a gold medal that tarnishes and fades. You're after one that's gold eternally. I don't know about you, but I'm running hard for the finish line. I'm giving it everything I've got. No sloppy living for me! I'm staying alert and in top condition. I'm not going to get caught napping, telling everyone else all about it and then missing out myself. 1 Corinthians 9:24-27 MSG

Keep yourself in training for a godly life. 1 Timothy 4:7b GNT

For the grace of God has appeared that offers salvation to all people. It teaches us to say "No" to ungodliness and worldly passions, and to live self-controlled, upright and godly lives in this present age. Titus 2:11-12 NIV

> Many people have great and grand desires that never materialize. They're missing the link between a dream and a reality—discipline. God has given you a free will to decide what you'll say "yes" to and "no" to. Good discipline brings desire into reality.

What God is speaking to me:

15

In faith and with a heart to obey, I confidently declare:

I am generous. I give freely. I give cheerfully. I love to give. I give abundantly. I give obediently. I give without expectations or strings. I have everything I need. I am content. I have plenty to give. I am blessed to be a blessing.

Give generously and generous gifts will be given back to you, shaken down to make room for more. Abundant gifts will pour out upon you with such an overflowing measure that it will run over the top! Your measurement of generosity becomes the measurement of your return. Luke 6:38 TPT

Remember that the person who plants few seeds will have a small crop; the one who plants many seeds will have a large crop. You should each give, then, as you have decided, not with regret or out of a sense of duty; for God loves the one who gives gladly. And God is able to give you more than you need, so that you will always have all you need for yourselves and more than enough for every good cause. As the scripture says, "He gives generously to the needy; his kindness lasts forever." And God, who supplies seed for the sower and bread to eat, will also supply you with all the seed you need and will make it grow and produce a rich harvest from your generosity. He will always make you rich enough to be generous at all times, so that many will thank God for your gifts which they receive from us. 2 Corinthians 9:6-11 GNT

I know how to live on almost nothing or with everything. I have learned the secret of contentment in every situation, whether it be a full stomach or hunger, plenty or want; for I can do everything God asks me to with the help of Christ who gives me the strength and power.
Philippians 4:12-13 TLB

But godliness with contentment is great gain. For we brought nothing into the world, and we can take nothing out of it. But if we have food and clothing, we will be content with that.
1 Timothy 6:6-8 NIV

Life can be lived with a mindset of scarcity or abundance. Scarcity defines life by limits—believing there's a fixed amount of resources to go around. When we think this way, we're prone to self-centeredness and tightfistedness. When we believe that resources are scarce, we grab for what we can get and hold dearly to what we have. An understanding of God's nature, of His never-ending supply and generosity, frees us to become generous, too. Part of growing in godliness includes growing in generosity.

What God is speaking to me:

16

In faith and with a heart to obey,
I confidently declare:

I put my trust in God, believing that He is good, faithful, able, powerful, and loving. He cares about me, concerns Himself with the things that concern me, is responsible for me and provides providential care over me. He is generous to me, desiring to bless me; never wanting to hurt or harm me. He has a purpose and plan for my life. He is completely and personally trustworthy.

You are good and do only good; make me follow your lead. Psalms 119:68 TLB

If you want favor with both God and man, and a reputation for good judgment and common sense, then trust the Lord completely; don't ever trust yourself. In everything you do, put God first, and he will direct you and crown your efforts with success. Proverbs 3:4-6 TLB

"For I know the plans I have for you," says the Lord. "They are plans for good and not for disaster, to give you a future and a hope." Jeremiah 29:11 NLT

And this same God who takes care of me will supply all your needs from his glorious riches, which have been given to us in Christ Jesus. Philippians 4:19 NLT

Relationships are built on trust. The greater the trust between people, the more potential for intimacy in the relationship. This is true with God. The quality of your relationship with Him will be determined, in large part, by the degree of trust you have in Him. Trust is created by trustworthiness. It comes from confidence in the character, integrity, and ability of someone. We can be confident in the goodness of God's character, His solid integrity, and His undeniable ability. This confidence in His trustworthiness allows us to trust Him with everything.

What God is speaking to me:

17

In faith and with a heart to obey,
I confidently declare:

I am liked, favored, accepted and loved by people. I have an ever-increasing circle of true friends. When I am disliked or rejected, I will not allow it to embitter me or rob me of love. I use these experiences to learn valuable lessons, gain insights about my life and relationships, and to become better, never bitter.

A man who has friends must himself be friendly, But there is a friend who sticks closer than a brother. Proverbs 18:24 NKJV

Two can accomplish more than twice as much as one, for the results can be much better. If one falls, the other pulls him up; but if a man falls when he is alone, he's in trouble. Also, on a cold night, two under the same blanket gain warmth from each other, but how can one be warm alone? And one standing alone can be attacked and defeated, but two can stand back-to-back and conquer; three is even better, for a triple-braided cord is not easily broken. Ecclesiastes 4:9-12 TLB

People learn from one another, just as iron sharpens iron. Proverbs 27:17 GNT

Don't just pretend to love others. Really love them. Never pay back evil with more evil. Do things in such a way that everyone can see you are honorable. Do all that you can to live in peace with everyone. Don't let evil conquer you, but conquer evil by doing good. Romans 12:9a, 17-18, 21 NLT

God wants you to have meaningful relationships. He'll bring people into your life as enduring friends, seasonal friends, and situational friends. Determine to be a good friend to others and choose wisely the friends you allow into your life. You'll also experience rejection along the way. Don't let the dislikes of others define your life. Learn from them and move on.

What God is speaking to me:

18

In faith and with a heart to obey,
I confidently declare:

I am controlled by faith, not by fear. God's perfect love for me drives out fear in my life. I give my worries to God and He gives me peace and works in all my concerns and challenges.

But in the day that I'm afraid, I lay all my fears before you and trust in you with all my heart. What harm could a man bring to me? With God on my side I will not be afraid of what comes. The roaring praises of God fill my heart, and I will always triumph as I trust his promises. Psalm 56:3-4 TPT

You will keep in perfect peace all who trust in you, all whose thoughts are fixed on you! Isaiah 26:3 NLT

Peace I leave with you; my peace I give you. I do not give to you as the world gives. Do not let your hearts be troubled and do not be afraid. John 14:27 NIV

For I am convinced that neither death nor life, neither angels nor demons, neither the present nor the future, nor any powers, neither height nor depth, nor anything else in all creation, will be able to separate us from the love of God that is in Christ Jesus our Lord. Romans 8:38-39 NIV

Don't worry about anything; instead, pray about everything; tell God your needs, and don't forget to thank him for his answers. If you do this, you will experience God's peace, which is far more wonderful than the human mind can understand. His peace will keep your thoughts and your hearts quiet and at rest as you trust in Christ Jesus. Philippians 4:6-7 TLB

For God has not given us a spirit of fear, but of power and of love and of a sound mind. 2 Timothy 1:7 NKJV

Where God's love is, there is no fear, because God's perfect love drives out fear. 1 John 4:18a NCV

We reach our highest potential and experience our greatest productivity in environments of faith and peace. This includes the internal environment of the heart and mind. God invites you to give your worries and fears to Him. He replaces it with confidence and peace so you can be your best for Him and others.

What God is speaking to me:

19

In faith and with a heart to obey,
I confidently declare:

I am an overcomer, a victor, a winner, a conqueror. I expect favor and good to come my way. My weaknesses make way for God's strength.

If you listen to these commands of the Lord your God that I am giving you today, and if you carefully obey them, the Lord will make you the head and not the tail, and you will always be on top and never at the bottom. Deuteronomy 28:13 NLT

No, in all these things we are more than conquerors through him who loved us. Romans 8:37 NIV

But he said to me, "My grace is sufficient for you, for my power is made perfect in weakness." Therefore I will boast all the more gladly about my weaknesses, so that Christ's power may rest on me. That is why, for Christ's sake, I delight in weaknesses, in insults, in hardships, in persecutions, in difficulties. For when I am weak, then I am strong.
2 Corinthians 12:9-10 NIV

And we know that God causes everything to work together for the good of those who love God and are called according to his purpose for them. Romans 8:28 NLT

We all love to win. Winning is an *attitude* before it's an event. Winners have a certain perspective on life. They celebrate life's victories. They also transform defeats into fertilizer for growth and development. This is the kind of attitude God wants you to cultivate and demonstrate.

What God is speaking to me:

20

In faith and with a heart to obey,
I confidently declare:

I work faithfully, wholeheartedly and with a positive attitude at whatever I am tasked to do. God blesses, multiplies and makes fruitful the work of my hands, the engagement of my mind and the inspiration in my spirit.

May the favor of the Lord our God rest on us; establish the work of our hands for us—yes, establish the work of our hands. Psalm 90:17 NIV

Do your best. Work from the heart for your real Master, for God, confident that you'll get paid in full when you come into your inheritance. Keep in mind always that the ultimate Master you're serving is Christ. The sullen servant who does shoddy work will be held responsible. Being a follower of Jesus doesn't cover up bad work. Colossians 3:23-25 MSG

God's favor is a powerful force. It creates opportunities and results for us that are beyond anything we could do for ourselves. The favor of God is an expression of God's love *for* us and grace *to* us. It's also a fruit of our commitment to certain attitudes and practices. When we bring our best to whatever we're assigned to do, God adds His favor.

What God is speaking to me:

21

In faith and with a heart to obey, I confidently declare:

I can do all things that God calls me to do through the power of Jesus Christ in me.

For I can do everything through Christ, who gives me strength. Philippians 4:13 NLT

The one who calls you is faithful, and he will do it.
1 Thessalonians 5:24 NIV

So do not throw away your confidence; it will be richly rewarded. You need to persevere so that when you have done the will of God, you will receive what he has promised.
Hebrews 10:35-36 NIV

What you attempt in life is determined by what you believe is possible. All of us are influenced by “can do” or “can’t do” thoughts. To fulfill God’s plan for your life, it’s important to aggressively replace the “can’t do” mindset with a “can do” way of thinking. Anything God asks you to do will be beyond your ability, but never beyond God’s ability.

What God is speaking to me:

22

In faith and with a heart to obey, I confidently declare:

I am a praiser, a worshiper, a grateful, honoring, and respectful person. I do not grumble, complain, belittle, or backbite.

Praise the Lord, my soul! Praise his holy name, all that is within me. Praise the Lord, my soul, and never forget all the good he has done. Psalm 103:1-2 GW

In everything you do, stay away from complaining and arguing so that no one can speak a word of blame against you. You are to live clean, innocent lives as children of God in a dark world full of people who are crooked and stubborn. Shine out among them like beacon lights, holding out to them the Word of Life. Philippians 2:14-16a TLB

In everything give thanks; for this is the will of God in Christ Jesus for you. 1 Thessalonians 5:18 NKJV

What kind of people do you enjoy being around—negative or positive? Negative people consistently spout complaints, frustrations and agitation. Positive people lift the atmosphere. They bring life by their words, attitudes, and interactions. You choose which you'll be.

What God is speaking to me:

23

In faith and with a heart to obey,
I confidently declare:

I don't have problems, I have opportunities for God's wisdom, grace and power to be demonstrated.

Dear brothers and sisters, when troubles of any kind come your way, consider it an opportunity for great joy. For you know that when your faith is tested, your endurance has a chance to grow. So let it grow, for when your endurance is fully developed, you will be perfect and complete, needing nothing. James 1:2-4 NLT

I have told you these things, so that in me you may have peace. In this world you will have trouble. But take heart! I have overcome the world. John 16:33 NIV

Take the old prophets as your mentors. They put up with anything, went through everything, and never once quit, all the time honoring God. What a gift life is to those who stay the course! You've heard, of course, of Job's staying power, and you know how God brought it all together for him at the end. That's because God cares, cares right down to the last detail. James 5:10-11 MSG

Let us not become weary in doing good, for at the proper time we will reap a harvest if we do not give up. Galatians 6:9 NIV

> Problems are ubiquitous and inevitable. You can't escape them, but you can successfully deal with them when you see them from God's perspective. With God, every obstacle and difficulty becomes an opportunity for answered prayer or personal growth. Usually it's both. When you change your perspective, you'll see there's a miracle in every mess and a testimony in every test of faith you experience.

What God is speaking to me:

24

In faith and with a heart to obey,
I confidently declare:

I am a diligent worker. I don't waste time. I invest my time wisely and fruitfully.

Lazy hands make for poverty, but diligent hands bring wealth. Proverbs 10:4 NIV

A hard worker has plenty of food, but a person who chases fantasies has no sense. Proverbs 12:11 NLT

A passive person won't even complete a project, but a passionate person makes good use of his time, wealth, and energy. Proverbs 12:27 TPT

Be very careful, then, how you live—not as unwise but as wise, making the most of every opportunity, because the days are evil. Ephesians 5:15-16 NIV

Your most precious resource is time. Once it's passed, it's past. You can't recover it. Your time is your life. Purposeful investment of time involves careful thought and planning, and deliberate action. Aimlessness, complacency and procrastination are the biggest thieves of time. God wants you to live with purpose, on purpose, without regrets. Take control of your time.

What God is speaking to me:

25

In faith and with a heart to obey,
I confidently declare:

I enjoy life and I rest well. I honor the Sabbath. I have the health, energy, and stamina to fulfill God's will and engage life joyously, enthusiastically, and vigorously.

For the joy of the LORD is your strength. Nehemiah 8:10b NIV

I sleep and wake up refreshed because you, Lord, protect me. Psalm 3:5 CEV

Then Jesus said, "Come to me, all of you who are weary and carry heavy burdens, and I will give you rest. Take my yoke upon you. Let me teach you, because I am humble and gentle at heart, and you will find rest for your souls. For my yoke is easy to bear, and the burden I give you is light."
Matthew 11:28-30 NLT

There is nothing better than for people to eat and drink and to see the good in their hard work. These beautiful gifts, I realized, too, come from God's hand. Ecclesiastes 2:24 Voice

If you watch your step on the Sabbath and don't use my holy day for personal advantage, if you treat the Sabbath as a day of joy, God's holy day as a celebration, if you honor it by refusing "business as usual," making money, running here and there—then you'll be free to enjoy God! Oh, I'll make you ride high and soar above it all. Isaiah 58:13-14a MSG

Now may God, the inspiration and fountain of hope, fill you to overflowing with uncontainable joy and perfect peace as you trust in him. And may the power of the Holy Spirit continually surround your life with his super-abundance until you radiate with hope! Romans 15:13 TPT

God created the world in six days. On the seventh day, He rested. God didn't rest because He was tired (He never grows weary). He rested as an example to us. Rest is an important part of a healthy life rhythm. We fool and harm ourselves when we ignore it. Rest starts on the inside. It's the result of trust. It also involves learning how to add "commas" and "periods" in our work life. A *refreshed* person is a *better* person in every area of life.

What God is speaking to me:

DALE A. O'SHIELDS

is the founding and senior pastor of Church of the Redeemer, a multi-cultural, multi-generational church with five campuses in the greater Washington, D.C. area.

Pastor Dale is passionate about inspiring people to grow in Christ and impact their church and community. His practical teaching makes the Bible understandable and applicable in everyday life. His messages are broadcast widely and he has written several books and devotional resources.

In over thirty years of ministry, Pastor Dale has trained and equipped pastors, nationally and internationally, to plant and develop strong and thriving ministries. He founded the United Pastors Network to regularly invest in church leaders and teams.

Pastor Dale has been involved in pastoral ministry since 1978. He and his wife Terry have two married daughters and seven grandchildren.

www.daleoshields.com